THE DECLINE AND FALL OF PUBLIC BROADCASTING

David Barsamian

SOUTH END PRESS
CAMBRIDGE, MASSACHUSETTS

Cover design by Ellen P. Shapiro

First printing.

Library of Congress Cataloging-in-Publication Data

Barsamian, David.
The decline and fall of public broadcasting / David Barsamian.
p. cm.
Includes bibliographical references and index.
ISBN 0-89608-654-2 (pbk.) ISBN 0-89608-655-0 (cloth)
1. Public broadcasting—United States. 2. Broadcasting policy—United States—Citizen participation. 3. Political participation—United States. 4. Internet—United States. I. Title.

HE8700.8 .B374 2001
384.54/06/5 21—dc21

Printed in Canada

2001049810

South End Press, 7 Brookline Street, #1
Cambridge, MA 02139-4146
www.southendpress.org

05 04 03 02 01 1 2 3 4 5

TABLE OF CONTENTS

"Become the media."

—Jello Biafra

"By not having to answer to the monster media monopolies, the independent media has a life's work, a political project, and a purpose: to let the truth be known. This is increasingly important in the globalization process. Truth becomes a knot of resistance against the lie."

—Subcomandante Insurgente Marcos,
La Realidad, Chiapas, January 31, 1997

FOREWORD

BY AMY GOODMAN

It is astounding what the public media have become in the United States. We have to reclaim our airwaves from the corporations and those who say they are protecting the airwaves in our name.

"Sesame Street" used to be brought to you by the number 2 and the letter A, which was sort of play on commercialism but not commercialism. Today "Sesame Street" is brought to you — and this is not a joke — by the number 2 and the letter Z for Zithromax by Pfizer. As David Barsamian argues in *The Decline and Fall of Public Broadcasting,* this is more and more what PBS is becoming.

These are very serious issues. It's not just kids who are being targeted and abused. It's adults, too.

We expect to be aware. We're very vigilant when it comes to commercial television. But we have to be very careful when it comes to public television, as well, which more and more is being shaped by corporate interests.

The media are so important in shaping the world today — more powerful than ever. Corporations like General Electric, Viacom, AOL Time Warner, and Disney are not just vast, wealthy businesses out to make a profit. They are trying to shape our worldview. They are the lens through which more and more people are seeing the world.

Is there any hope? Yes. And, and as Barsamian demonstrates, it's independent media. We saw it rise up, not first, but most spectacularly in Seattle, when tens of thousands of people took to the streets in a remarkable moment, a turning point at the end of the century. People who cared came together and simply said No. This was a global uprising against corporate power.

Hundreds of people from around the world also said that this uprising against corporate power is not going to just be seen through a corporate lens. They came together with pens and pencils, tape recorders, and video cameras, and created the Independent Media Centers.

What the elites fear more than anything is the globalization model happening from below, from the grassroots, rather than from above — and that is happening right now.

There are solutions. The solution is all of us banding together and saying, We're not only going to fight for equality and social justice, but we're going to make sure that there are media there that are getting the word out and presenting an honest account of our issues.

It's critical that we support the independent media, but also that we continue to challenge corporate media and demand that they open up their ranks.

In *The Decline and Fall of Public Broadcasting,* David Barsamian not only shows us how we can take steps together to achieve a more democratic media, but how urgent it is that we do.

WATCHDOGS OR LAPDOGS?

The future of public broadcasting is more important than ever. Why? Because our sources for news and information are becoming more and more limited. Thomas Jefferson said, "The information of the people at large can alone make them safe." What will happen to democracy if a handful of corporations own, mint, and distribute that information? This is an issue that citizens should be deeply concerned about. Monopoly control of media and the means to deliver information are serious threats to democracy.

In Orwell's *1984,* inconvenient history and facts were thrown "down the memory hole" at the Ministry of Truth, where they were burnt and irrevocably forgotten.[1] The 1967 Carnegie Commission Report (CCR), the founding document for public broadcasting in the U.S. has, alas, met such a fate. Before shining light into the hole and retrieving some valuable information, let's first look at the overall context of the media.

In 1983, Ben Bagdikian wrote his classic book on media concentration, *The Media Monopoly,* published by Beacon Press in Boston, one of the few independent presses left in the United States. Bagdikian, a mainstream journalist who is dean emeritus of the Graduate School of Journalism at the University of California at Berkeley, said that fifty corporations dominated the media in the United States. If you look at the reviews of his book from that time, he was criticized for being hyperbolic and for not having faith in the free-market economy to create more and more alternatives.

In 1987, Bagdikian came out with the second edition. Fifty companies had become 28. A few years after that, in 1990, 28 had become 23. And then 14 in 1992. By 1997 the number was 10. And in the latest edition, which came out in 2000, the number is down to six.

It sounds like an Agatha Christie story — then there were nine, then there were eight, then there were six. Six corporations dominate and control the media. And, Bagdikian says, "Their intricate global interlocks create the force of an international cartel." He adds, "Power over the American mass media is flowing to the top with … devouring speed."[2] As concentration accelerates, waves have turned into electronic tsunamis crisscrossing and hard-wiring continents. In fact, Bagdikian points out,

> The power and influence of the dominant companies are understated by counting them as "six." They are intertwined: they own stock in each other, they cooperate in joint media ventures, and among themselves they divide profits from some of the most widely viewed programs on television, cable, and movies.

They constitute what he calls a "private ministry of information."[3]

The outcomes that Bagdikian describes are happening because the two political parties and governmental agencies are basically captives of the media corporations and genuflect before them.

For example, when he came into office, President George W. Bush appointed Michael Powell — the son of Secretary of State Colin Powell — as chair of the Federal Communications Commission. The

FCC, which is in charge of regulating the nation's airwaves and defending the archaic notion of "the public interest," is run by someone who believes, in Powell's words, that there's "too much regulation, too much government interference in telecommunications."[4] This is from someone who, when asked about the extreme inequality in access to Internet technology — the so-called digital divide — said, "I think there is a Mercedes divide. I'd like to have one; I can't afford one."[5]

According to the *Financial Times,* Powell

> advocates the view that regulators should be striving to interfere as little as possible in the operations of the market. A former competition lawyer, Mr. Powell promotes an agenda "that could easily work him out of a job." Powell explains, "I have a greater confidence in proper market structure as a way of disciplining market behavior. We don't believe in deregulation for its own sake."[6]

This is totally laughable. There has been minimal U.S. government regulation of telecommunications. A 25-year-old rule prohibiting networks from owning two TV stations in the same city was overturned in 1999. "It's going to be a land rush to some degree," one media executive told the *New York Times* when the decision was made.[7] On April 19, 2001, the FCC voted to end the "dual network" rule, which had prevented one television network from buying another.[8] Almost on cue, three months later, Rupert Murdoch's News Corporation, which also owns The *New York Post,* was allowed to acquire a second TV station in New York, the country's largest media market.[9]

Powell recently called media conglomerates "our clients."[10] And for the class interests he represents, that is accurate. For once, we have truth in high places.

The New Deal–era politicians who created the FCC in 1934 viewed the communications infrastructure as a vital public resource, like utilities or the railroads. The agency was originally charged with protecting consumers from industry monopolies and price gouging. But a September–October 2001 *Mother Jones* article, "Losing Signal" by Brendan I. Koerner, exposes an emergent corporate-friendly FCC, as embodied by Powell.[11] Among Powell's first actions was an April 2001 decision to relax regulations prohibiting companies from owning multiple broadcast networks. This change allowed Viacom, which merged with CBS in 2000, to continue as owner of UPN. A few weeks earlier, Powell had expedited the approval of 32 radio-station mergers. In addition, Powell has said he will review the important "cross-ownership" rule, which prevents companies from owning a newspaper and television station in the same region.

"On these and other far-reaching questions, the agency's positions are shaping up to be virtually identical to the ones being drawn up in corporate boardrooms," writes Koerner. Powell dismissed the FCC historic mandate to evaluate corporate actions based on the public interest at an American Bar Association (ABA) panel discussion in spring 2001. That standard, he said, "is about as empty a vessel as you can accord a regulatory agency."

The *Mother Jones* story also dramatically illustrates the impact of corporate lobbying on the FCC's decision making. Koerner reports that the lobbying expenses of the communications industry stand at about $125 million per year, more than twice the amount spent on similar efforts by the defense industry. And disclosure filings confirm that FCC commissioners and staff spend a great deal of time hearing from corporate representatives in meetings called "*ex parte* proceedings." *Mother Jones* reviewed the records for 43 such meetings from June 4, 2001, to June 7, 2001, and found that "[a]t least 38 of those sessions were with lobbyists from SBC, AT&T, WorldCom, and other corporate interests." Public interest advocates, the article notes, don't have the staff or money to match their presence.

Furthermore, FCC commissioners and staff frequently come from corporate backgrounds or move on to lucrative private sector jobs. For instance, in the late 1980s, Dennis Patrick, who is now the president of AOL Wireless, was chair of the FCC. Powell's predecessor, William Kennard, worked at the influential Washington-based law and lobbying firm Verner Liipfert, before heading the agency. Verner Liipfert is known for its powerful communications practice.

While the FCC is little more than a rubber stamp for its clients, it does find time to limit free speech and play censor. It brought obscenity charges against KBOO, the Portland, Oregon, community radio station. KBOO's crime? It played Sarah Jones's "Your Revolution," a defiant and brilliant song that is a response to misogyny-laden gangsta rap. "Your revolution will not happen between these thighs," Jones sings. KBOO faces a $7,000 fine and legal fees.[12] The enormous power of the state is brought to bear upon a small, independent, community radio station.

Ralph Nader is one of the few people who remind us that the nation's airwaves belong to the people. In the current deplorable structure, that simple fact is stood on its head. We the people, the landlords, are treated as tenants. The insult doesn't stop there. We are subjected to programming that is vacuumed of content, that presents a range of opinion from A to B, from GE to GM. Bruce Springsteen wrote a song, "57 Channels (And Nothin' On)." Soon he will have to add a zero to that "57."

In the early 1960s, Newton Minow (John F. Kennedy's FCC Commissioner) used the term "vast wasteland" to characterize the commercial media.[13] What words would he find today as we are inundated with coverage of Chandra Levy, Elian Gonzalez, Jon-Benet Ramsey, and the latest shark attacks?

While Minow's "vast wasteland" comment barely survives, the rest of his remarkable speech has been deep-sixed. In his address to the National Association of Broadcasters, the major commercial radio and television lobby, he repeatedly referred to the "public's airwaves." He noted that "the squandering of our airwaves is no less important than the lavish waste of any precious natural resource." He urged his audience "to put the people's airwaves to the service of the people." Minow unambiguously stated that "the people own the air. They own it as much in prime evening time as they do at six o'clock Sunday morning. For every hour that the people give you, you owe them something."[14]

The commercial airwaves are instruments for profiteering. The TV and radio networks deliver eyeballs and ears to other profiteers, that is, advertisers. Those advertisers want to market their products to consumers with the money to buy their wares. The media are driven by advertising dollars, not the 50 cents you or I pay at the newsstand. That's another reason why corporate interests dominate the airwaves and why media conglomerates get a free ride from the government.

These conditions present severe obstacles to democratic discourse. Jefferson's rather radical idea was that the citizenry needed a wide range of opinion to flourish and engage in the democratic process. Instead, we are confronted with the bleak outcomes that Bagdikian documents in *The Media Monopoly*.

Corporate-owned and -operated microphones and digital cameras limit public discourse.

Today the media — both so-called public and private — saturate us with propaganda generated by the golden Rolodex experts from the Cato Institute, the American Enterprise Institute, the Hudson Institute, the Manhattan Institute, and the Heritage Foundation. These pundits are recycled on program after program. Some, like Mark Shields, move effortlessly from the PBS "NewsHour" to CNN, as does Cokie Roberts from her perch on NPR's "Morning Edition" to ABC. The latter, incidentally, speaks in front of groups that she covers. Her speaking fee is in excess of $20,000.[15]

Public broadcasting, established in 1967 during the Johnson Administration, was supposed to be different. The founding charter, written by powerful U.S. businessmen and philanthropists, called for the public broadcasting system to *"be a forum for debate and controversy"* and "provide a voice for groups in the community that may otherwise be unheard."[16]

But constant political interference, highly centralized and conservative organizational structures at PBS and NPR, and an over-reliance on corporate money have undermined the original mission. You can turn on the TV and see for yourself what PBS has turned into: a steady stream of cooking shows, Lawrence Welk re-runs, British comedies, studies of insects mating, nightly business reports, "Antiques Road Show," and African animals — without Africans. In June 2001, PBS announced that it was adding the UK-based version of "Antiques Roadshow" to its line-up.[17]

NPR has evolved from its early days, when it had a raw, cutting-edge quality, to being predictable and ever so polite. In the first broadcast of "All Things Considered" on May 3, 1971, reporters covered massive demonstrations in Washington, D.C., against the Vietnam War. There were live reports from the streets, the kind of improvisational journalism that the Independent Media Centers are doing now in the United States, Europe, and elsewhere. Today, NPR and PBS journalists go to officialdom for comments, not to the nongovernmental organizations, the grassroots groups, or the demonstrators.

The role of media in general — particularly public media — should be adversarial. Reporters, should go, in the words of Amy Goodman, "to where the silences are."[18] There once was an adage that the function of journalism was to "comfort the afflicted and afflict the comfortable."[19] Today, most journalists comfort the comfortable and afflict the afflicted. They have become overpaid stenographers to power who compete for the best hair on the air. Instead of watchdogs, they are lapdogs.

Notes

1 George Orwell, *1984* (New York: Knopf, 1992).
2 Ben H. Bagdikian, *The Media Monopoly,* 6th ed. (Boston: Beacon Press, 2000), p. viii.
3 Bagdikian, *The Media Monopoly,* p. 1.
4 Dan Roberts, "FCC Chief 'Working Himself Out of a Job,'" *Financial Times,* May 25, 2001, p. 3.
5 Clarence Page, "FCC's Powell Must Help Close 'Digital Divide,'" *Newsday,* February 12, 2001, p. A22.
6 Roberts, "FCC Chief 'Working Himself Out of a Job.'"
7 *New York Times,* August 6, 1999.
8 Fairness and Accuracy In Reporting, "FCC Moves to Intensify Media Consolidation," April 20, 2001: http://www.fair.org/activism/cross-ownership.html.
9 Peter Spiegel, "FCC Approves News Corp TV Purchases," *Financial Times,* July 26, 2001, p. 22.
10 Michael K. Powell, Testimony, Hearing of the Telecommunications and Internet Subcommittee of he House Energy and Commerce Committee, Washington, DC, Federal News Service, March 29, 2001.
11 Brendan I. Koerner, "Losing Signal," *Mother Jones,* September–October 2001, p. 41–44, 90–91.
12 See Chris Merrick, "F.C.C. vs. KBOO," on-line at http://www.kboo.org/about/fcc.htm. The lyrics to the song are at http://www.kboo.org/about/fcc.htm#lyrics. Sarah Jones, "Your Revolution," *DJ Vadim* (Ninja Tune).

13 Newton Minow, Speech to the National Association of Broadcasters, May 9, 1961.

14 William Hoynes, *Public Television for Sale: Media, the Market, and the Public Sphere* (Boulder: Westview Press, 1994), p. 39.

15 See Jill Abramson, "For Capital Pundits, Money for Speeches Is Scarce This Year," *New York Times,* November 28, 1997, p. A1.

16 Ralph Engelman, *Public Radio and Television in America: A Political History* (Thousand Oaks, California: Sage Publications, 1996), p. 2; emphasis added.

17 Elizabeth Jensen, "PBS Shuffles the Deck, Moving Key Series to New Time Slots," *Los Angeles Times,* June 8, 2001, p. 6: 25.

18 Amy Goodman, speech at Grassroots Radio conference, July 14, 2001, Boulder, Colorado. Available from Alternative Radio.

19 Finley Peter Dunne, American journalist, 1902.

THE DECLINE AND FALL OF PUBLIC BROADCASTING

Public radio and public television enjoy "liberal" reputations, but if you come to the evidence without prejudice, you'll overwhelmingly find that's simply not the case. On PBS, for instance, the established, syndicated programs include "Wall $treet Week," "Washington Week in Review," "The Nightly Business Report," "NewsHour with Jim Lehrer," which is on every night of the week, "The Charlie Rose Show," which is also on nightly, "Tony Brown's Journal," "Ben Wattenburg's Think Tank," and "Talking Money with Jean Chatzky." The official name of "Masterpiece Theatre" is actually "ExxonMobil Masterpiece Theatre."

The longest running program in public affairs in PBS history was William Buckley's "Firing Line," which was aired for more than three decades. The program was mercifully discontinued in 2000.

John McLaughlin, formerly of the right-wing *National Review* magazine, occupies a unique place on PBS. He has not one, but two shows: "The McLaughlin Group" and "One on One." How this man commands two public affairs programs on PBS is mind-boggling. Though he has little talent other than his penchant for bombast, his ability to attract long-time corporate funding from General Electric and Archer Daniels Midland is undoubtedly a factor in his prominence at PBS.[1]

On public radio — including not only NPR, but also Public Radio International — you hear business programs like "Marketplace" and "Sound Money." Guest commentators on "All Things Considered" and "Morning Edition" are far more likely to come from the right than the left. Content analysis of these programs will definitely reveal a bias, but not in the liberal direction. It's decidedly conservative.

According to a study done by Fairness and Accuracy in Reporting (FAIR), "Representatives of organized citizen groups and public interest experts made up only 7 percent of NPR sources — about the same found in earlier FAIR studies of 'Nightline' and 'MacNeil/Lehrer.'"[2] A decade or so ago the likes of Erwin Knoll, Michael Harrington, and Molly Ivins were regular commentators on NPR and PBS. Where are comparable voices today?

As Susan Douglas, a media analyst at University of Michigan and the author of *Listening In: Radio and the American Imagination,* observes,

> Progressive voices are heavily censored.... Where is the one show on television that's the progressive week in review, that would have Matt Rothschild or Katha Pollitt or Salim Muwakkil or Barbara Ehrenreich? They are interesting and lively people. This could be great television. But who's going to sponsor it?
>
> You have the same thing on radio. NPR used to feature a range of voices and opinions from people from the left to the middle to the right. Now you really struggle to hear people from the left on NPR.... I think NPR knows that all you have to do is get one or two of these voices on and a small, and I mean small, but very vocal and influential minority, will start raising hell about the left-wing bias of NPR.

Douglas also points to the lack of stories about working people in public television and radio:

> Labor? Do we have a working class in this country? You don't see or hear them.... The dominant image of the labor union ... is some fat, corrupt bureaucratic institution. There's no countervailing imagery that shows what working-class life is like.... What we see and hear is an upper middle-class white view of the world that represents probably five percent of the population. The rest have been forgotten. I was just thinking about this recently as I was looking once again at Studs Terkel's book *Working.* What a great radio program that would be, a show called "Working." What's it like to be a chambermaid? What's it like to manufacture candy in a factory. What's it like to build bridges?... It's a whole side of life that has been censored, that is forbidden.[3]

Garrison Keillor, whose radio show "A Prairie Home Companion," is a staple on hundreds of public radio stations, despairs at the direction NPR has taken:

> I think "All Things Considered" has gotten terribly soft in recent years. We're all very, very polite toward each other in public radio. But I think we have to speak the truth from time to time.

> "All Things Considered" made its reputation on news reporting during the Watergate episodes. They produced a generation of excellent reporters. Nina Totenberg is still there. Cokie Roberts has mostly moved on to television and lecturing and all. Bill Buzenberg has moved on. John Hockenberry has moved on. These are tremendous people who gave you first-class reporting on radio. They've mostly been overshadowed by what I consider to be rather precious commentators, people reminiscing about their childhoods and interviews with artists and writers who one sort of gathers are friends of the reporters. A lot of things just don't add up.

As Keillor notes:

> This is an urgent question because of the precipitous decline in newspapers in this country, which is evident to anyone who travels around the country and reads. Newspapers in this country are falling apart. As a result, most people in this country do not live within range of a serious newspaper, a good newspaper, that really intends to deliver the world to you. This places an obligation on public radio.
>
> Public television never accepted that it had any journalistic responsibility whatsoever. Local

> public television has never done anything by way of news, with very few exceptions. The "MacNeil/Lehrer NewsHour" sort of goes back and forth from analysts and analysis and interviews to something more like hard news.
>
> Radio has a real obligation here, and I think that "All Things Considered" has seriously failed this obligation in recent years. I think the program has for one thing utterly failed to report on the Republican revolution that took control of Congress that has absolutely turned politics upside down in this country.
>
> This is not a minor phenomenon. I don't know if reporters at NPR simply don't know Republicans, or they don't know how to talk to them, or what. But this is a crucial story. It goes on under their noses. To ignore that and to do little audio documentaries about old ballplayers and celebrate Paul Robeson's birthday and do a documentary on maple syruping in Vermont is just perverse.

Keillor does not spare PBS, either:

> I don't think there's any reason for public television to exist any more.... They are so far from being an important force in broadcasting, and

> their accomplishments are so far in the past. There isn't anything that they do that can't be done and done better by any one of a dozen cable channels. They've been completely rendered obsolete by cable television. Public television came up when there were three commercial networks and maybe there was another station in town that showed old movies. Then it meant something. But they're a complete dinosaur. What C-SPAN is now is what public television should have been and never had the wit to do.[4]

According to Public Radio International's *Program Source* magazine, "When Garrsion Keillor talks, people listen in the millions"[5] — except, that is, when he is voicing criticisms of PBS and NPR.

Similar concerns to Keillor's have been raised by former higher ups at PBS. Before quitting, PBS program chief Kathy Quattrone complained, "Many program decisions are being based not on the program value they bring but what kind of a deal it can bring." Former PBS President Bruce Christensen has warned that, unless the funding problems can be solved, public broadcasting "will become a commercial medium in the next century."[6]

The origins of the commercial and conservative bias on public television and radio go back to the late 1960s, when public broadcasting was established. At the time, Japan and Europe had already developed well-funded radio and television networks. So the U.S. came to the game rather late, in 1967, with a Corvair-like design, structurally flawed from its inception.

The Carnegie Commission Report — considered "the single most important document in the history" of public broadcasting — was written by such establishment luminaries as James R. Killian, Jr., head of MIT, who also served as its chair; James B. Conant, the president of Harvard University; and Edwin H. Lamb, the CEO of Polaroid. Their proposal unequivocally stated that the United States should have a publicly funded, non-commercial public broadcasting service. The Carnegie report envisioned programming that would "provide a voice for groups in the community that may otherwise be unheard" and "help us see America whole, in all its diversity."[7]

The Carnegie Commission Report was the foundation for the creation of what are now the

Public Broadcasting Service (PBS) and National Public Radio (NPR).

Within nine months of the Carnegie report, Congress overwhelmingly passed the Public Broadcasting Act of 1967. Encouraging its passage was President Lyndon Johnson, who said that "the public interest be fully served through the public airwaves."[8] In the legislation adopting the Carnegie recommendations, Congress created the Corporation for Public Broadcasting (CPB), a nonprofit, nongovernmental corporation. CPB is the conduit for federal monies, which provides funding support to more than 1,000 public television and radio stations across the country. It does not produce programs, but with its hand on the till, it wields considerable power and influence over public broadcasting.

The Public Broadcasting Act called for an "alternative" broadcast system that would express "diversity and excellence," involve "creative risks" and address "the needs of unserved and underserved audiences." The act called for "programs of high quality obtained from diverse sources," that would be "made available to *non-commercial* educational television and radio broadcast stations."[9]

The Carnegie report also proposed that funding for this new entity be protected from political influence. The report foresaw that if the purse strings were controlled by Congress, then their independence would be threatened, stating: "We would free the Corporation to the highest degree from the annual governmental budgeting and appropriations procedures: the goal we seek is an instrument for the free communication of ideas in a free society."[10] However, Congress rejected the commission's advice to provide forward funding for public broadcasting. A so-called "heat shield" was necessary to protect the nascent network from the vagaries of appropriations, but Congress would have none of it. It wanted to keep the new endeavor on a tight leash.

Compare this to the how public broadcasting systems all over the world are funded, whether through television and radio taxes or licensing fees. Broadcast airwaves are the only public resources that are given away for free. Citizens for Independent Public Broadcasting (CIPB) has a sound and imaginative proposal about how this could be done in the United States.

Because the "broad mix of Congressional and legislative appropriations, subscriber donations and corporate and foundation underwriting" that U.S. public broadcasting relies on forces public broadcasters to "play it safe," CIPB supports the establishment of an independently funded public trust, comparable to "the Red Cross." The trust would "replace the President's patronage-appointed" CPB and "take over the satellite distribution systems now administered by PBS and NPR." Most importantly, the body would be staffed by representatives of the public broadcasting and educational communities. The board would be insulated from direct political pressure, and funding would be set up to encourage public affairs programming.[11]

Instead, in the United States, from its inception, the relatively small budget of the public broadcasting system has been hostage to Congress and the White House.

It didn't take long for PBS to start taking hits. In 1970, it aired a documentary called "Banks and the Poor," which critically examined banking practices that exacerbated poverty in urban areas.[12] The program closed with a list of 133 senators and representatives with bank holdings or positions on the boards of directors of banks. This sent President Nixon into a tizzy, and in June 1972, he vetoed the two-year funding bill for public broadcasting.[13] The chair, president, and director of PBS resigned before Nixon eventually changed his mind and signed the bill. But the message was conveyed. The vulnerability of the system had been exposed.

In fact, virtually since its inception there has been constant political pressure to temper public broadcasting and to control its content. One method has been through "flak," consistently pressuring public radio and television through the incessant canard that they have a left-wing bias. It started with Nixon in the 1970s. In the 1980s, NPR was accused of being "Radio Managua on the Potomac." In the next decade, PBS was denounced by David Horowitz as a forum for "the discredited pro-Soviet left."[14] And it continues today. In August 2001, the extreme right-wing group CAMERA (the Committee for Accuracy in Middle East Reporting in America) absurdly accused NPR of "extreme anti-Israel partisanship," despite coverage by reporters such as Linda Gradstein, whose sympathies for Israel are blatant.[15] (For example, in 2001, during the Al-Aqsa Intifada, Gradstein said, "I think Israel has to retaliate," in response to a question from "Morning Edition" host Renee Montagne.[16])

The persistence of the charge of PBS/NPR left-wing bias truly tests the imagination and requires someone of Jonathan Swift's ability to do justice to it. The formidable right-wing propaganda apparatus nevertheless constantly circulates this shibboleth.

Funding for public broadcasting has been compromised from the very beginning, and deliberately so. The Corporation for Public Broadcasting (CPB) was set up by Congress to be a nongovernmental agency that would funnel money to public television and radio stations. CPB members are appointed by the president, thus insuring political influence. Robert T. Coonrod has been the president and CEO of the CPB since 1997. Prior to joining CPB, Coonrod was deputy managing director of the Voice of America, the propaganda agency of the U.S. government. (Not to be outdone, NPR's president and CEO Kevin Klose served as the director of the International Broadcasting Bureau, which oversees VOA, RadioFree Europe, Radio Liberty, and Radio and Television Marti.[17]) Television journalist Bill Moyers appropriately warns, "What is emerging is not public television but government television shaped by politically conscious appointees whose desire to avoid controversy could turn CPB into the Corporation for Public Blandness."[18] Since the inception of public broadcasting, Congress and the White House have, with few exceptions, been long on the political attack and short on the financial support. The predictable result is that PBS and NPR have been driven into the outstretched arms of corporate advertisers. Public broadcasting's elite audience is, as they say on Madison Avenue, a "most desirable demographic" and much coveted by image conscious corporations.

NPR boasts that it "serves a growing audience of more than 15 million Americans each week via 620 public radio stations and the Internet and in Europe, Asia, Australia and Africa via NPR Worldwide, to military installations overseas via American Forces Network, and throughout Japan via cable."[19]

In its pitch to potential advertisers, PBS encourages businesses to:

> Learn how PBS Sponsorship can help your corporate message stand out from the clutter of commercial advertising — and reach *your* target audience! Through sponsoring PBS programming such as Talking Money with Jean Chatzky, Clifford the Big Red Dog, and Washington Week, you not only build your brand and en-

> hance your marketing, you also become associated with the high public image of PBS.

Most importantly, "Compared to the broadcast and cable networks, PBS viewers tend to be more affluent, better educated and more likely to be opinion leaders." Put simply, "You reach those with purchasing power."[20]

In addition to boasting about how its advertising reaches children ("Children Watch More PBS than Other Networks," one chart explains), PBS adds:

> A national sponsorship on PBS is an integrated marketing communications package. PBS sponsorship extends beyond the screen, with targeted communications to key audience segments. From home videos, to companion books, promotions and outreach programs like teacher's guides, your sponsorship message is substantially enhanced beyond the television screen.[21]

Advertising on PBS has also provided corporations with the added fillip of damage control. For example, PBS — which is sometimes called the Petroleum Broadcasting Service because of the huge amount of support it gets from big oil companies —

has been an ideal vehicle to deflect reports of record profits, charges of price gouging, and negative publicity related to environmental disasters like the Exxon *Valdez* spill in Alaska.[22]

The grain giant Archer Daniels Midland (ADM) is an instructive example. The "Supermarket to the World" has now morphed into "The Nature of What's to Come." ADM is a long-time advertiser on PBS's "NewsHour." In 1995, the company was convicted of price-fixing lysine on the international market. The story was front-page news in the *Wall Street Journal* and *New York Times,* and made the cover of *Fortune.*[23] However, during that entire year, there was only one report on the scandal on the "NewsHour."[24] As the journalist James Ledbetter points out, "ADM has been the single largest recipient" of federal subsidies. ADM averages some $4 billion a year slurping at the public trough. Program host Jim Lehrer says his show's coverage "has absolutely nothing to do with who is and who isn't an underwriter."[25] ADM has also been a big advertiser on NPR.

The marked development of commercialization of both public television and radio is certainly counter to the spirit and the letter of the 1967 Public Broadcasting Act. It is also important to note that the legislation used the word "alternative" to describe the system Congress was creating. Again, these inconvenient facts are buried deep in the Memory Hole.

As a result of funding pressures, NPR and PBS have become entrepreneurs, as local radio stations themselves. WBUR Radio in Boston sponsors trips, including East African safaris. PBS stations sell tote bags, DVDs, CDs, and books because these products bring in money and individual donors. If you visit NPR's web site, you can go to Shop NPR, which tells you: "Our wide selection of clothing, CDs, mugs and other unique items make great holiday gifts for everyone. Browse through fashionable, top-quality products and take advantage of our easy-to-use ordering system."[26]

But far more important is the fact that producers and executives sell programming to generate support from corporations, a major source of income that is euphemistically called "underwriting." Underwriting is an Orwellian term for advertising, and as underwriting of public radio and television has increased, so has the airtime given to corporate underwriters. The proliferation of ads has drawn the wrath of *New York Times* commentator Walter Goodman.

He writes, "advertising of any sort runs smack against the ideal of public broadcasting as an oasis in a desert of marketing." He decries "the commercials that have grown like sores on this purportedly non-commercial endeavor." The ads "are an insult to the viewers' intelligence" and put "the nation on notice that public broadcasting in the United States is fated never to be able to make it in an unadulterated form."[27]

PBS had $12.9 million in operating earnings in fiscal year 2000. It received $175.9 billion in program underwriting, $50.5 million in "educational product sales," and $81.7 million in royalties, license fees, investment income and other sources of income. Compare this to the $43.7 million it received in CPB and U.S. Department of Education grants. In the fine print, you can read how "Total revenue excludes strategic partners' direct investments in specific program projects which contributed $29 million in fiscal 2000, $10 million in fiscal 1999, $7 million in fiscal 1998, $15 million in fiscal 1997 and $5 million in 1996."[28]

As the PBS 2000 Annual Report explains,

> PBS continues to leverage resources from its member stations and the Corporation for Public Broadcasting (CPB) with growth in private-sector alliances, grants and entrepreneurial revenues.... Operating revenues grew 60 percent, or $118 million, from fiscal 1996 to fiscal 2000, primarily through non-station sources such as video sales, licensing, cable royalties and U.S. Department of Education grants.

When PBS first started underwriting, corporate sponsors could only be identified by their name. Nothing could be said about qualifying who they were or what they produced. Thus, "Masterpiece Theatre" was "brought to you by the Mobil Corporation." That all changed when Reagan came to Washington. In 1983, "enhanced" underwriting was introduced, thus ushering in full-fledged advertisements, which are particularly ubiquitous on PBS.

If you listened to NPR at the beginning of 2001, during the tenth anniversary of the Gulf War, you heard the following underwriting announcement. "The State of Kuwait, in memory of the tenth anniversary of Kuwait's liberation. On the web at Kuwait Thanks America dot org."[29] According to NPR's ombudsman, Jeffrey Dvorkin, NPR received "about

$170,000" to run the announcement.[30] While Dvorkin maintains that there is a "firewall" between NPR's business operations and its news department, practice belies theory. (Kuwait's NPR underwriting produced so much public protest that it decided to discontinue the practice of accepting money from foreign governments.)

At the same time as the Kuwait ads were running, NPR was covering the Gulf War anniversary. Colin Powell repeated the official U.S. story that the ten-year-old embargo on Iraq, which has claimed hundreds of thousands of civilian lives, did not bar humanitarian goods from the country. But at the time, more than $3.5 billion worth of goods, overwhelmingly humanitarian items badly needed for Iraq to have functioning medical, electrical, and water sewage systems, were being blocked by the United Nations sanctions committee, mostly because of U.S. veto power. Powell's assertions went unchallenged by NPR.[31]

Distorted coverage of Iraq has a history. In 1990, in the lead-up to the Gulf War, the totally fabricated Kuwaiti incubator story was aired on PBS and NPR.[32] A bogus Congressional hearing was organized by Hill & Knowlton, one of the country's largest public relations firms. A tearful young eyewitness named Naira claimed she was working in a hospital when Iraqi troops burst in. She testified, "They took the babies out of incubators, took the incubators, and left the babies on the cold floor to die."[33]

The impact of this story did much to galvanize public support for the Desert Storm assault on Iraq. There were a couple of problems with the tale. First of all, it was a caucus, not an official Congressional hearing. But much more than that, Naira was not in Kuwait when the incident supposedly happened, and she was the daughter of the Kuwaiti Ambassador to the U.S., Saud al-Sabah, and a member of the ruling Sabah family. An investigation later revealed that Hill & Knowlton was in the employ of none other than the Kuwaiti government. When all of this was later revealed, the "NewsHour," which originally ran the story, did not air a retraction.[34]

Not to be outdone by their commercial brethren, PBS and NPR program hosts and reporters also suffer from acute "we"-itis, a deadly journalistic disease. They identify so closely with state power that they adopt the collective pronoun, as when PBS's Margaret Warner asked in 1998, "Should we be trying to oust Saddam Hussein?"[35]

An egregious example of non-reporting occurred in September 2001. The *Progressive* ran a powerful exposé that month about the deliberate destruction of Iraq's water supply system by the United States. George Washington University School of Business and Public Management professor Thomas Nagy unearthed official documents from the Defense Intelligence Agency,

> proving beyond a doubt that, contrary to the Geneva Convention, the U.S. government intentionally used sanctions against Iraq to degrade the country's water supply after the Gulf War. The United States knew the cost that civilian Iraqis, mostly children, would pay, and it went ahead anyway.[36]

Another example of the questionable firewall between advertising and reporting took place in March 2001 on "Morning Edition," hosted by Bob Edwards. On March 14, an underwriting credit from Merrill Lynch, a major investment firm, was immediately followed by a discussion on the bear market and the decline of high-tech stocks. The financial experts interviewed by Edwards advised listeners to shift to more safe, secure, and conservative investments.[37]

Who is funding public radio and TV? Archer Daniels Midland, ExxonMobil Corporation, Metropolitan Life, Salomon Smith Barney, and other Fortune 500 companies. The following corporations and organizations gave more than $1 million to PBS in the 2000 fiscal year:

Fiscal Year 2000 Underwriters of PBS National Programming: $1 Million and Above[38]

A.G. Edwards & Sons, Inc.
A.T. Kearney
AARP (American Association of Retired Persons)
Ace Hardware Corporation
Alfred P. Sloan Foundation
American Society for Microbiology
Ameritech Corporation
Archer Daniels Midland Company
Arthur Vining Davis Foundations
Barnes & Noble, Inc.
Chase Manhattan Corporation
Chevrolet Motor Division
Chubb Group of Insurance Companies
CNET, Inc.

Eastman Kodak Company
ExxonMobil Corporation
Fidelity Investments
First Union Corporation
Ford Foundation
J. Willard & Alice S. Marriott Foundation
John D. and Catherine T. MacArthur Foundation
Kellogg Company
Lilly Endowment, Inc.
LookSmart Ltd.
Metropolitan Life Insurance Company
Minwax Company
Mutual of America
National Endowment for the Arts
National Endowment for the Humanities
National Science Foundation
New York Life Insurance Company
Northwestern Mutual Life Insurance
Oppenheimer Funds, Inc.
Park Foundation
PeopleSoft, Inc.
Pfizer Inc.
Salomon Smith Barney, Inc.
Saturn Corporation
SBC Communications, Inc.
State Farm Mutual Automobile Insurance Company
toysmart.com

Travelers Insurance Companies
U.S. Department of Education (via Corporation for Public Broadcasting)
Verizon Communications

These leading "donors" are major corporations that have a huge investment in the economy, and can use their economic power to leverage program content. Independent producers who approach PBS and NPR for airtime get a much warmer reception when they have an underwriting package in hand. Overwhelmingly, programs that will attract and please corporate underwriters and crucially, won't rock the ideological boat, get access to the airwaves.

Here and there, programming that challenges conventional wisdom gets on PBS or NPR, such as Bill Moyers's "Surviving the Good Times," about two families in Milwaukee affected by plant closures during the highly celebrated U.S. "miracle economy" in the 1990s, or the occassional probing documentary on "P.O.V." But they are the exception and are increasingly infrequent.

Corporate advertising poses one set of problems for public broadcasting. The ideological and political climate that informs the content of programs is yet another concern. A mandarin caste of milquetoasts at each station — only a handful of people, and sometimes just one individual — decides what gets on the air. They are acting as gatekeepers, deciding what we will see and hear.

Let me give you some examples. In 1993, PBS aired "The Prize: The Epic Quest for Oil, Money, and Power," a series funded by Paine Webber, a company with petrochemical oil interests.[39] The main analyst of the series was Daniel Yergin, a consultant to major oil companies. Almost every expert featured was a defender of the oil industry. That same year, PBS aired a documentary called "James Reston: The Man Millions Read," a rather flattering profile about the *New York Times* columnist. The film was funded by and produced in association with the *New York Times,* Reston's long-time employer. The director and producer of the film was Susan Dryfoos, a member of the Sulzburger family, which owns the *New York Times,* and the daughter of a former *Times* publisher. Conflict of interest? Fahggeddaboudit.

Occasionally, you may see a cutting edge documentary on your local PBS station, like Jeremy Brecher and Tim Costello's film, narrated by Edward Asner, on the race to the bottom in labor and environmental standards caused by globalization. "Global Village or Global Pillage?" aired on Connecticut Public Television in 2000, but has not been shown in other markets.[40] If PBS doesn't give something its benediction for national broadcast, then it's unlikely that individual stations will break from the network and broadcast a progressive documentary.

Certainly the issue is not a lack of quality programming. In 1995, an Academy Award–winning documentary short on domestic violence by Margaret Lazarus and Renner Wunderlich, "Defending Our Lives," was rejected at PBS. "Defending Our Lives" was filmed in Framingham Prison for Women in Massachusetts and focused on eight women prisoners who had been battered and beaten by the husbands they eventually killed. One of the producers was a leader of a battered women's support group, but PBS felt that this gave her "a direct vested interest in the subject matter of the program" — perhaps because she was against domestic violence. PBS added that "programming must be free from the control of parties with a direct self-interest in that content."[41]

PBS also declined to air a documentary called "The Money Lender$: The World Bank and IMF," a film by Robert Richter.[42] Why? PBS was concerned that "Even though the documentary may seem objective to some, there is a perception of bias in favor of poor people who claim to be adversely affected."[43]

PBS also turned down "Out at Work," an excellent film about gays in the workplace that was shown at the Sundance Film Festival. The film, produced and directed by Kelly Anderson and Tami Gold, was scheduled to be part of the series "Point of View" ("P.O.V.") before PBS dropped it.[44] One of the subjects of the film is a woman named Cheryl Summerville, who was fired as a cook from a Cracker Barrel restaurant outside Atlanta in 1991 for "failing to comply with normal heterosexual values." Another subject in the film worked as an electrician at Chrysler.

"We found 'Out at Work' to be compelling television responsibly done on a significant issue of our times," PBS Director of News and Information Programming Sandra Heberer wrote. But, she added, "PBS's guidelines prohibit funding that might lead to an assumption that individual underwriters might have exercised editorial control over program content — even if, as is clear in this case, those underwriters did not."[45] Which underwriters? It turns out that 23 percent of the program's $65,000 budget came from Astraea National Lesbian Action Foundation and a number of labor unions. The message is unambiguous. Corporations can fund projects, but unions and civil rights organizations cannot.

Another fine documentary that should be much more widely known is "Paying the Price: Killing the Children of Iraq" by John Pilger, an award-winning Australian-born, British-based journalist, which is about the impact of sanctions. But "Paying the Price" will not be shown on PBS. Nor will Pilger's film on East Timor, "Death of a Nation."

"In Search of Palestine," a 1998 film by Edward Said produced by the BBC, has disappeared in the United States, virtually unseen. In the United Kingdom, by contrast, it has been shown all over. A few years earlier, Said was featured in "The Idea of Empire," another BBC production. It was also not aired in the United States. PBS cannot argue that Said is an unknown entity. A veritable Renaissance figure, his books *Orientalism* and *Culture and Imperialism* serve as the bookends to postcolonial studies.[46] He is also without question the foremost advocate for Palestinian rights in this country, which, no doubt, creates problems for the skittish nabobs at PBS.

"Stories My Country Told Me," featuring the scholar and human rights activist Eqbal Ahmad, has never been on PBS, nor has "Zapatista!" a film about the movement in Chiapas.[47] There's a fabulous series on the drug war called "Dealing with the Demon" by the Australian Broadcasting Corporation, which has also never shown on PBS.

Danny Schechter, a renowned independent producer, wanted to do a series called "Rights and Wrongs: Human Rights Television." Charlayne Hunter-Gault, a prominent African-American reporter who had served for years as a national correspondent for PBS's "MacNeil/Lehrer NewsHour," was to be the anchor. When Schechter approached PBS program director Jennifer Lawson with his proposal, she turned him down, saying that human rights was "an insufficient organizing principle" for a series.[48]

As Schechter is quick to respond, "And cooking shows do? And 'Wall $treet Week' does? That's what PBS is all about?"[49] Schechter had to undergo the arduous task of pleading with individual stations to air the series. This episode evokes the sagacious words of the great social commentator Lily Tomlin, "No matter how cynical you get, it's almost impossible to keep up."

Eventually, Schechter succeeded in getting the program on some stations. "Rights and Wrongs" won a string of awards, but, strapped for funding, it was discontinued.

In 2000, Haskell Wexler and Johanna Demetrakas made a documentary called "Bus Riders' Union," about organizing bus riders in Los Angeles. It's also not been aired on PBS, even as California has undergone a massive energy crisis that exposes the need for more public transportation. Your best chance of seeing the video is to watch it on the World Wide Web.[50] Wexler, a multiple Academy Award–winner, famous cinematographer and documentary filmmaker, recipient of the American Society of Cinematographers' Lifetime Achievement Award, should get a special prize for having the most documentaries rejected by PBS. Starting with his Academy Award–winning "Interview with My Lai Veterans," through "Brazil: A Report on Torture" and "Target Nicaragua: Inside a Secret War," right up to the present day.

Two more Academy Award–winning documentaries that PBS shunned are Barbara Trent's "The Panama Deception" and Debra Chasnoff's "Deadly Deception: GE, Nuclear Weapons, and our Environment." It almost seems that an Academy Award is a disqualification as far as PBS program decision makers are concerned.

Two films have been made on the Seattle/WTO uprising, one called "Showdown in Seattle: Five Days That Shook the WTO," and the other called "This is What Democracy Looks Like." Again, neither has been broadcast.[51] And a multiple award-winning documentary about Noam Chomsky called "Manufacturing Consent" has never been nationally sponsored and distributed by PBS, though it has had screenings around the world.[52]

That's just a partial list. Occasionally things do slip through like the occassional Bill Moyers documentary, but in the aggregate, the odds are stacked against getting a program on PBS if it goes against conventional wisdom. "Tales of the City," an award-winning dramatic series, was very popular, earning higher ratings than most PBS programs. But because the main characters were gay, it came under attack from the right wing and it was dropped.[53]

Ironically, HBO picked it up and developed it into an even more successful series.

But most of the censorship occurs before a program sees the light of day. The people who actually make programming decisions have very narrow ideas about what should be on the public airwaves. The same is true of "All Things Considered" and "Morning Edition," the flagship NPR daily news programs, which have audiences in the millions. On many stations, these shows are rolled over repeatedly. For example, Colorado Public Radio (CPR) begins "Morning Edition" at 4 a.m. and runs it until 10 a.m. In the afternoon, CPR airs "All Things Considered" at 3 p.m. and runs it until 7.

CPR is typical of a trend in NPR-member stations. There is virtually no local programming and anything remotely progressive has little chance of getting on the air. Stations around the country download off the satellite hours and hours of NPR and, to a lesser extent, PRI programming. It's a no-brainer for the program directors. Just flip the switch to the big bird in the sky and pump the signal onto the air. The dominance and prevalence of NPR's "All Things Considered" and "Morning Edition" rest as much on their bulk — each program is two hours long — as on their non-controversial and "safe" content.

"All Things Considered" and "Morning Edition" are literally the bread and butter for many stations because they are aired during drive time when listenership is at its highest. But they come at a very high price to stations. NPR charges them hefty fees. Hence, the constant on-air and off-air fundraisers, as well as the pursuit of corporate money. At most stations, so-called development departments — that is, professional money chasers — have larger budgets and staff than the news departments. That's certainly the case for public television stations, where local news is almost non-existent.

Progressive programs face enormous obstacles to getting on the air, even when, like Alternative Radio (the program I produce), they are offered to stations free. They would rather broadcast a game show like "Wait! Wait! Don't Tell Me" or a business program like "Marketplace."

For example, despite being called "the conscience of the American people," Noam Chomsky is almost never heard on NPR.[54] If you leave your radio on, every ten years you might hear Chomsky. It's rather startling that he and many other progressive voices are never heard on the premier public radio network in the country. Robert Siegel, a longtime host of "All Things Considered," made his prejudices fairly well known a few years ago when he wrote that Chomsky "evidently enjoys a small, avid and largely academic audience who seem to be persuaded that the tangible world of politics is all the result of delusion, false consciousness and media manipulation."[55]

The lengths to which NPR has gone to marginalize Chomsky are particularly revealing given his international stature and ability to draw huge audiences wherever he speaks. Cynthia Peters, a former long-time editor at South End Press, experienced this first hand when she tried to get some coverage for Chomsky after the publication of his 1988 book *The Culture of Terrorism.*[56] Peters said she "had been amazed at how little attention Chomsky got in the mainstream press. With the publication of *Culture of Terrorism,* I made it my personal mission to get Chomsky, and his message, some mainstream airtime." Peters contacted Margaret West, a producer at "All Things Considered," and set up an interview with Chomsky. On the day the interview was scheduled to air, West called Peters and told her to listen for it between 5 and 5:30 p.m. At the top of the hour, "All Things Considered" announced its line-up for the coming half hour, including the Chomsky interview.

> The half hour ticked by, and those of us gathered around the radio in the South End Press office were stunned as we realized that — as the bottom of the hour drew nearer and nearer and still no interview — that somehow someone had made a last-minute decision to punt it....
>
> At around 25 minutes past the hour — during the last possible segment for the interview — NPR played a whole lot of segue music and made some meaningless announcements. It was clear, they were using filler for the dead time caused by the suddenly missing Chomsky interview.

When Peters called "All Things Considered," West said, "It aired, just like I told you it would." Eventually, West called back and acknowledged that the program's producer, Neal Conan, listened to the segment and decided that the interviewer had not sufficiently challenged Chomsky.[57] Without consulting West, he employed a rarely used veto, and pulled the interview off the program at the last minute. As Peters observers,

> Chomksy's ideas are so far outside the scope of what is considered acceptable debate by the mainstream media, that NPR was willing to pay a fairly high price to cut him out of the line-up. Margaret West, the interviewer, and everyone else in the newsroom who was paying attention learned an important lesson that day.
>
> Better to cut a wide berth around Chomsky. Failure to learn from such experiences likely leads to getting fired or demoted. This is one of the ways journalists learn to censor themselves.

"All Things Considered" did finally air an interview with Chomsky, but "one they believed made him look properly marginal," Peters says. "In the end, he had a very brief amount of on-air time — maybe two minutes."[58]

PBS is even worse. When Katharine Kean from Crowing Rooster Art submitted the documentary "Haiti: Killing the Dream" to PBS in 1992, she was asked, "Who is Noam Chomsky and what does he know about Haiti?"[59]

In more than 25 years of the "NewsHour," Chomsky was on only once, in 1990.[60] An interesting project would be to compare the number of times Chomsky has been on international media outlets like BBC and CBC (Canadian Broadcasting Company), where he is a frequently quoted and respected commentator, with his U.S. appearances.

Radical voices are simply excluded from public discourse. They do not exist. They're not on the "NewsHour with Jim Lehrer." They're never interviewed by Charlie Rose. On the rare occasions Rose has had Edward Said on, he does not let him finish a sentence. There's a torrent of, "What about, what about?" Yet when Rose has perennial favorites like Thomas Friedman or Henry Kissinger on, he genuflects and exhibits proper awe and reverence. He has turned sycophancy into an art form.

Rose permits Friedman, a repeat guest, endless time to promulgate at length his theories on the Middle East without challenging them. For example, Friedman, with Rose chiming in agreement, repeated the claptrap about the incredibly generous Israeli offer at Camp David in 2000 and how, once again — won't he ever learn? — Arafat lost a great opportunity.[61]

Rose and NPR's Bob Edwards face stiff competition for champion bore. If there were a statute of limitations, then all these guys, including Jim Lehrer, would have been off the air years ago. Lehrer is in his third decade on PBS's nightly public affairs show. Some dub his show "The SnoozeHour."

The state of public broadcasting in the United States can be disheartening. But there are some very important and positive developments. There are a series of high quality programs that simply did not exist five, ten, or twenty years ago. Programs like "Democracy Now!" (now in exile), "Making Contact," "CounterSpin," "Alternative Radio," "T.U.C.," "Women's International News Gathering Service," "Radio Nation," "Free Speech Radio News," and "Independent Native News."

There is also a growing microradio and community radio movement, despite tremendous obstacles. A group in Ft. Collins, Colorado was recently awarded a frequency, but only after a seven-year struggle. Microradio is also sometimes called "pirate radio," but since the airwaves are public, we should ask who the real pirates are: independent community broadcasters or big corporations who get a free ride and have hijacked the airwaves and inundate us with pabulum?

Radio stations are extremely valuable properties, particularly in the commercial band. The demand for bandwidth has increased significantly, particularly since the Telecommunications Reform Act of 1996 was ushered through with the fervid support of Clinton and Gore. As Chomsky says, whenever you hear the word reform, you should reach for your wallet.[62] The act, one of the greatest giveaways in U.S. history, raised the caps on the number of stations that one entity can own in a particular market, dramatically changing the country's electronic landscape. Defenders of capitalism talk about "a level playing field." Well, how level is a field in which it's you versus News Corporation, Viacom, and AOL Time Warner? No matter what your politics are — whether you are conservative, liberal, or radical — it's not arguable that homogenization is the order of the day. Listeners have commented that when they drive across the country they hear the same songs everywhere. That's not surprising, given the extensive use of computerized play lists and formats.

But microradio activists are trying to break the corporate juggernaut. If you want to start your own microradio station, you can get a kit from Free Radio Berkeley and become a broadcaster.[63] A lot of people have been doing that, much to the chagrin of the National Association of Broadcasters (NAB) and NPR. Astonishingly, in 2000 NPR formed an alliance with NAB to block the licensing of microradio stations. According to the *New York Times,* "National Public Radio prevailed with the assistance of the commercial broadcasters" in putting a bill through Congress that overturned an FCC ruling that would have allowed the licensing of microradio. As the *Times* explained,

> Tucked away in legislation that Clinton signed was a provision sought by NAB and NPR that sharply curtails Federal Communications Commission plans to issue licenses for low-power FM radio stations to 1,000 or more schools, churches and other small community organizations.
>
> The provision, by setting new technical standards and repealing those already determined by the FCC, makes it all but impossible for licenses to be issued in cities of even modest size.... The FCC's low-power radio plan was conceived last January to counter the huge consolidation in the broadcasting industry that the agency's chairman, William E. Kennard, con-

cluded had led to a sharp decline in the diversity of voices on the airwaves. Kennard saw the plan as a cornerstone of his agenda to promote civil rights issues at the FCC....

"This is a resource that everyone has to share," Kennard said in an interview. "We can't allow people who have the spectrum to use their political clout to shut out voices that don't have the same clout. This highlights the power of incumbency. Companies that have spectrum guard it jealously, and they can use Congress to prevent new voices from having access to the airwaves."[64]

This is a serious blow for democracy.

Notes

1 On GE sponsorship of the McLaughlin Group, see the program's web site at http://www.mclaughlin.com/. On ADM, see "Brought to You By...," *Extra!* (October 1993). On-line at http://www.fair.org/extra/best-of-extra/public-tv-conservatives.html.

2 Fairness and Accuracy In Reporting (FAIR), "Study Finds National Public Radio Fails To Reflect Public," Press Release, March 29, 1993. Available on-line at http://www.fair.org/reports/npr-study.html.

3 Susan J. Douglas, "Talking Heads," Alternative Radio, September 22, 2000, San Diego, California. Transcript available from AR at http://www.alternativeradio.org/. See also Susan J. Douglas, *Listening In: Radio and the American Imagination, from Amos'N'Andy and Edward R.*

Murrow to Wolfman Jack and Howard Stern (New York: Times Books, 1999).

4 Garrison Keillor, Interview with David Barsamian, November 14, 1997, Boulder, Colorado. Available from Alternative Radio.

5 *Program Source* 19: 8 (September 2001), p. 2.

6 Citizens for Independent Public Broadcasting (CIPB), "The Crisis of U.S. Public Broadcasting": http://www.cipbonline.org/propintro.htm.

7 Carnegie Commission on Educational Television, "Public Television: A Program for Action," on January 26, 1967: http://www.current.org/pbpb/carnegie/CarnegieISummary.html. See also John Carmody, "Carnegie Commission II Finds 'Fundamental Flaws' in the Public Broadcasting Setup," *Washington Post,* January 30, 1979, p. B1.

8 William Hoynes, *Public Television for Sale: Media, the Market, and the Public Sphere* (Boulder: Westview Press, 1994), p. 39.

9 Hoynes, *Public Television for Sale,* p. 13.

10 Carnegie Commission on Educational Television, Summary. See notes 6 and 7 above.

11 See CIPB, "The CIPB Proposal for a Public Broadcasting Trust": http://www.cipbonline.org/trustMain.htm.

12 National Educational Television Center (NET), "Banks and the Poor." PBS, November 9, 1970.

13 Hoynes, *Public Television for Sale,* p. 3.

14 David Horowitz, "The Politics of Public Television," *Commentary* (1991), pp. 25–32.

15 See Ali Abunimah, "CAMERA's Continued Assault on NPR and the Truth," The Electronic Intifada, August 21, 2001. On-line at http://electronicintifada.net/features/mediaonmedia/orgcommentary.html. The report, "A Record of Bias: National Public Radio's Coverage of the Arab-Israeli Conflict," September 26–November 26,

2000, is at http://world.std.com/~camera/docs/report/nprrecord.html.

16 NPR, "Morning Edition," August 9, 2001.

17 Neal Conan, "NPR President," "All Things Considered," PBS, November 11, 1998.

18 James Day, *The Vanishing Vision: The Inside Story of Public Television* (Berkeley: University of California Press, 1995), p. 231.

19 See NPR's web site: http://www.npr.org/about/.

20 "Benefits of PBS Sponsorship," available on the secure web site at http://sponsorship.pbs.org/.

21 "Sponsorship Package Elements," available on the secure web site at http://sponsorship.pbs.org/.

22 See Brian Tokar, *Earth for Sale: Reclaiming Ecology in the Age of Corporate Greenwash* (Boston: South End Press, 1997).

23 Scott Kilman and Bruce Ingersoll, "Risk Averse," *Wall Street Journal,* October 27, 1995, p. A1, and Kurt Eichenwald, "Executives Said to Describe Illegal Pay at Grain Company," *New York Times,* September 26, 1995, p. A1.

24 Robert MacNeil, "The MacNeil/Lehrer NewsHour," PBS, August 8, 1995.

25 James Ledbetter, *Made Possible By: The Death of Public Broadcasting in the United States* (New York: Verso, 1998), p. 156.

26 Available on-line at http://shop.npr.org/.

27 Walter Goodman, "Now a Word from Our Spon ... uh,um ... Our Friend," *New York Times,* October 19, 1999, p. E2.

28 PBS 2000 Annual Report. Available on-line at: http://www.pbs.org/insidepbs/annualreport/summary.html.

29 "Between Feb. 12 and March 4, 2001, NPR aired underwriting credits from the government of Kuwait as it marked the 10th anniversary of its liberation from Iraq. Three years ago, NPR accepted underwriting from the

German government to commemorate the anniversary of the collapse of the Berlin Wall." Siriol Jane Evans, Senior Manager, Public and Media Relations, NPR, Private Correspondence, March 16, 2001. See also Bob Edwards, "Celebration Marking the Tenth Anniversary of Kuwait's Liberation from Iraqi Occupation," "Morning Edition," NPR, February 26, 2001, and Robert Siegel, "Kuwait Holds Ceremonies to Celebrate Tenth Anniversary of the End of the Persian Gulf War," "All Things Considered," NPR, February 26, 2001.

30 Amy Goodman, Interview with Jeffrey Dworkin, "Democracy Now!" March 14, 2001.

31 Scott Simon, "Colin Powell to Travel to Middle East in an Effort to Get Support for UN Sanctions Against Saddam Hussein," "Weekend Edition," NPR, February 10, 2001.

32 Robert MacNeil, "The MacNeil/Lehrer NewsHour," PBS, December 18, 1990; John Alcott, "Opposing Saddam," "The MacNeil/Lehrer NewsHour," PBS, March 5, 1991; and Robert Siegel, "Human Rights Committee Heard Iffy Data on Iraq," "All Things Considered," NPR, January 6, 1992.

33 John MacArthur, *Second Front: Censorship and Propaganda in the Gulf War,* 2nd ed. (Berkeley: University of California Press, 1993), pp. 58–59.

34 Confirmed by an analysis of Lexis-Nexis transcripts.

35 Margaret Warner, "Toppling Hussein," "The NewsHour with Jim Lehrer," PBS, November 25, 1998.

36 Thomas Nagy, "The Secret Behind the Sanctions: How the U.S. Intentionally Destroyed Iraq's Water Supply," *The Progressive* 65: 9 (September 2001).

37 Bob Edwards, "Investors Shifting to Safer Portfolio Strategies," "Morning Edition," NPR, March 14, 2001.

38 PBS 2000 Annual Report. On-line at http://www.pbs.org/insidepbs/ annualreport/supporters.html.

39 http://www.fair.org/press-releases/pbs-factsheet.html, FAIR, "Public Television?"

40 See Jeremy Brecher, Tim Costello, and Brendan Smith, *Globalization from Below: The Power of Solidarity* (Cambridge: South End Press, 2000), and the video Brecher, Costello, and Smith co-produced, *Global Village or Global Pillage? How People Around the World Are Challenging Corporate Globalization* narrated by Edward Asner (available from South End Press).

41 Tara Gadomski and Esben Kjaer, "PBS: The Decline and Fall of 'Public' Broadcasting," The Consortium. On-line: http://www.consortiumnews.com/archive/story39.htm l. Cambridge Documentary Films, Margaret Lazarus.

42 An updated version of the video is now available. See the video's web site at http://www.richtervideos.com/d_money.html.

43 See Mark Mori and Joan Sekler, "Counterpunch: The Public Gets Shut Out of 'Reinvented' Public TV," *Los Angeles Times,* January 10, 1994, p. F3.

44 http://artcon.rutgers.edu/papertiger/news/pbs.html

45 Janine Jackson, "Film Rejection Highlights PBS Bias," *Extra!* (January–February 1998). Available on-line at http://www.fair.org/extra/9801/pbs-film-reject.html.

46 Edward W. Said, *Orientalism* (New York: Random House, 1979), and Edward W. Said, *Culture and Imperialism* (New York: Vintage Books, 1994).

47 David Barsamian, *Eqbal Ahmad: Confronting Empire* (Cambridge: South End Press, 2000).

48 Norman Solomon, "The Media Wrongs of Human Rights," Creators Syndicate, October 23, 1996.

49 Jerold M. Starr, *Air Wars: The Fight to Reclaim Public Broadcasting* (Boston: Beacon Press, 2000), p. 238.

50 http://www.slickpictures.com/credits_bus_riders.html.

51 http://www.whisperedmedia.org/showdown.html.

52 http://www.zeitgeistfilm.com/catalogue/manufacturing consent/manuconsent.html.

53 See Stephen M.H, Braitman, "He Still Has Plenty of Tales to Tell," *Los Angeles Times,* May 10, 1995, p. E1.

54 "Prophet Without Honour: Noam Chomsky," *The Independent* (London), January 11, 1989, p. 27.

55 Robert Siegel, "Chomsky: Not Cutting Edge," Letter to the Editor, *Current,* January 16, 1995, p. 22.

56 Noam Chomsky, *The Culture of Terrorism* (Boston: South End Press, 1988).

57 Noam Chomsky, *Language and Politics,* ed. Carlos P. Otero, David (Montreal: Black Rose Books, 1988), pp. 506–07.

58 Author correspondence with Cynthia Peters, August 2001.

59 Author correspondence with Katharine Kean, August 2001.

60 Robert MacNeil, Interview with Noam Chomsky, "MacNeil/Lehrer NewsHour," PBS, September 11, 1990.

61 See, among other examples, Charlie Rose's interview with Friedman on January 2, 2001.

62 Noam Chomsky and David Barsamian, *Propaganda and the Public Mind: Conversations with Noam Chomsky* (Cambridge: South End Press, 2001), p. 215.

63 For more information, see the Free Radio Berkeley web site at http://www.freeradio.org/.

64 Stephen Labaton, "Congress Severely Curtails Plan for Low-Power Radio Stations," *New York Times,* December 19, 2000, p. A1.

INDEPENDENT MEDIA ALTERNATIVES

A series of initiatives have been undertaken that counter the negative developments I have described so far. For example, Michael Albert, a co-founder of South End Press and of *Z* magazine, has created an online information resource called Z Net. It enables people who are doing countercultural work in the media to do an end run around the corporate print press and to reach large numbers of people. Every day Z Net sends out incisive commentaries on issues of the day. In the last several years, Z Net has signed up 3,000 paid "sustainers," not just in the U.S. but all over the world ("from Nepal to the Bronx," in Albert's words). More than 50,000 e-mail commentaries go out every day. The web site has 85,000 unique sessions a week. According to Albert, the service has helped put *Z* magazine and the Z Media Institute in "the best financial situation they've ever been in," showing the tremendous interest in alternative viewpoints that is not being met by existing media institutions.

As Albert says, "We wanted to use the web to get information out and simultaneously build interactive community." Z Net provides a model, but Albert also notes that "unless progressive audiences realize the need to financially support alternative media far more than they are currently doing, many projects may suffer losses, rather than gains, due to the influence of the web."[1]

Another development that is taking place outside of PBS is a dramatic miniseries based on Howard Zinn's best-selling book *A People's History of the United States*. Because of the politics of public broadcasting, the series is now being produced by HBO, the cable network. Despite backing from Hollywood stars Matt Damon and Ben Affleck, Zinn decided that approaching PBS with the project would be a waste of time. "The two producers who took options on *A People's History of the United States* to do a series of documentaries based on it both agreed, on the basis of their own experience, that they would not try to get PBS to do the project," Zinn explained.

"They had heard from many people in the field that PBS was fearful of anything that might be considered radical, and they thought a cable company, and even the commercial networks, would have more courage than PBS to undertake such a project."

Zinn also drew lessons from his own experiences with public television and radio. In 1991, after the Soviet Union had disintegrated, he was called by the "MacNeil/Lehrer NewsHour," asking if he would take part in a panel to discuss the future of socialism after the fall of the Soviet Union. Zinn agreed. He was then asked off-air for a summary of his views.

> I said it would be a big boost for socialism, since the Soviet Union had given socialism a bad name by pretending to embody it, and that with the Soviet Union out of the way, it might be possible to restore the good name of socialism, the idealism, the vision of a truly democratic society, that had led millions in this country, and many more abroad, to embrace the idea of socialism. Well, I never heard from the program again.

The panel did take place, with Zinn replaced by James Weinstein, who was then the editor of *In These Times* magazine. As Zinn notes,

> Weinstein was cynical, pessimistic, and felt that the fall of the Soviet Union signaled a decline in the prospects for socialism. It seemed to me that the program was looking for just that viewpoint, and found my approach not what they wanted.[2]

Other important projects have not appeared on PBS and NPR for the simple reason that producers don't feel the effort is worth it. In addition, more and more young people are taking to heart Jello Biafra's call to "Become the Media." They aren't just criticizing and complaining about the mainstream media; they're producing their own. This is very important not just for political reasons but also psychologically. While it is crucial to have an ongoing critique and understanding of corporate media, we have to produce alternatives.

Independent Media Centers (IMCs) are springing up all over the United States and around the world. They been instrumental, if not in reversing the tide of globalization, certainly in putting some roadblocks in its path. IMCs played a prominent role not only in organizing but in disseminating information about major demonstrations that took place during the past few years in Prague, Seattle, Washington, D.C., at the Republican convention in Philadelphia, and the Democratic convention in Los Angeles. They provided a demonstrator's-eye-view of these historic events with live and archival coverage that you couldn't see on television or read about in your local paper.

Independent media organizing has a long history. During the 1960s, underground newspapers, film collectives, and radio newswires were instrumental in bringing about political change and reached millions of people. Organizations like the Detroit-based Dodge Revolutionary Union Movement not only put out their own paper, they helped make an independent documentary film about their struggle.[3] But indy media has experienced a renaissance since mass demonstrations shut down the World Trade Organization's ministerial meetings in Seattle, Washington, in November 1999.

In Seattle, more than 400 Internet, print, photo, radio, and television journalists converged to create an ad hoc newsroom and called it the Independent Media Center. Its goal was to make sure that protesters would not be silenced by corporate-owned media outlets and that the corporate media's version of events, "all the news that's fit to print," would not be the only one. The IMC produced up-to-the-minute coverage throughout the week of the protests.

When CNN, citing official police sources, reported that no rubber bullets were fired in Seattle, the IMC posted photos and video of the actual rubber bullets fired into crowds of clearly nonviolent demonstrators. The IMC web site was flooded with hits that day, and CNN had to change its story.[4]

Since Seattle, IMCs have multiplied around the globe. Currently, around 60 IMCs are in operation across five continents.

"Of course, IMC prospects aren't all sunny," notes Eric Galatas, of Free Speech TV, a progressive television network based in Boulder, Colorado, who has worked closely with the IMCs.

> Nearly two years into a non-hierarchical and consensus-based experiment, a formal decision making policy has yet to be adopted. More importantly, IMCs face the challenge of balancing the ratio of privileged and mostly white indy media contributors with youth, women, and people of color. A real commitment is essential to cre-

> ate IMCs that more accurately reflect the diversity of the communities most impacted by neoliberalism. And fundraising prospects are grim, in part due to a recent MacArthur Foundation decision to cut support for media centers. Who to turn to, when the only public funds available for media are reserved for corporate-friendly operations like PBS and NPR?[5]

In spite of these hurdles, the IMC print team is now publishing a regular distillation of reports from international affiliates. This weekly two-page document is available in five languages. It's published as a PDF file, which means that anyone with access to the Internet can become their own printing press.[6]

These are exciting intiatives taking place outside of corporate control. Independent presses like Odonian, Seven Stories, South End, and others are publishing radical books that are selling in large numbers. That's very encouraging. This is all the more remarkable as these books have virtually no publicity, and receive few reviews, even in the left press. A whole series of CDs with Angela Davis, Howard Zinn, and Noam Chomsky has also sold in the thousands. A lot of these digital recordings are circulating like *samizdat* in the old Soviet Union. MP3 technology is allowing for distribution in informal networks. New technologies are helping countercultural ideas reach a young audience that's completely turned off to NPR and PBS.

And while it is difficult to get on public radio and public television, you can do it, particularly outside the iron corridor that runs from Boston to Miami. In the rest of the country, it's somewhat easier to break through. So it's possible to get on the air in states such as Colorado and New Mexico. My program, Alternative Radio (AR), is aired on Montana Public Radio. One would think AR would be on in "liberal" Boston and have no chance at all in Montana, but it's just the opposite.

While there are several hundred NPR-type stations airing predictable fare, the U.S. has a fairly sophisticated community radio network. These stations range from big cities like Tampa to small towns like Astoria, Oregon. Many of these stations are also reaching out beyond their broadcast range through streaming audio over the Internet. There are some excellent stations you can listen to now through this medium. The station that I'm rooted in, KGNU in Boulder, one of the best in the country, has a great mix of music, information, and news. You can now listen to it online. You can also hear WMNF in Tampa, Florida, and KUNM in Albuquerque, New Mexico, on the web.

If you want to hear "Democracy Now!" or "Making Contact," you can find out what time they're broadcasting on a particular station and tune into the live feed. Or you can often go to the show's web site and listen to archived broadcasts.

Another encouraging development in community broadcasting is grassroots radio. The Grassroots Radio Coalition (GRC) mission statement speaks about building the "cornerstones of participatory democracy." As the statement explains, "More than audio outlets, volunteer-based community radio stations are cultural institutions in their communities, reflecting the unique concerns and passions of the people who live there."

> The grassroots radio movement in the United States grew organically within community radio as it became evident that community radio was falling prey to the negative forces of commercialization, corporatization, and homogenization which have infiltrated so much of the media,

says Marty Durlin, station manager at KGNU in Boulder, "including public broadcasting."

The CPB has cut back support for such community broadcasting efforts, notably ending a provision that credited stations for volunteer hours worked at the station. "By rewarding the creation of new funding sources, including 'enhancing' and increasing underwriting and creating profit-making ventures," Durlin explains, "CPB shifted the burden of financial support away from listeners and federal funds and toward the commercial sector."

In response to these pressures, grassroots activists have tried to organize themselves to effectively counter the homogenization of the public airwaves. A network of community radio stations hosted the first Grassroots Radio Conference in Boulder, Colorado, in 1996, and have organized a series of successful gatherings since. The first conference had 85 participants, the second had more than 100, and the third had 130. Some 160 people participated in the 2000 gathering.[7]

Such positive developments are also being extended into public television. Since May 2000, Free Speech TV (FSTV), the first full-time, progressive television channel in the United States, has broadcast 24 hours a day, seven days a week on Echostar's Dish Network. FSTV's roots are in the 90s Channel, started by John Schwartz, which broadcast into selected markets as a paid access station on the TCI cable system (now a part of AT&T). TCI's John Malone eventually forced the channel off the air through huge rate increases. After a failed legal battle, Mallone and others regrouped and launched FSTV in 1995, providing four hours a week of social documentaries to a network of 50 public access cable channels. Today, through a combination of its public access and dish outlets, FSTV estimates it reaches at least 10 million homes in the United States.

"The work of progressive producers and filmmakers that is censored or screened out from PBS and corporate television is seen on Free Speech TV," explains Brian Drolet, Internet director for FSTV in Boulder. "Most significantly, FSTV provides a new national venue for grassroots organizations and activists."[8] Like the IMCs, FSTV has played an important role in broadcasting news from protests around the globe, including live coverage of the protests at the Republican and Democratic conventions in Philadelphia and Los Angeles in 2000.

FSTV plans to go on the road with a mobile studio in 2002, bringing stories that might otherwise be largely unheard to a national television audience.

Notes

1. Author correspondence with Michael Albert, August 2001.
2. Author correspondence with Howard Zinn, July 2001.
3. Dan Georgakas and Marvin Surkin, *Detroit: I Do Mind Dying: A Study in Urban Revolution* (Cambridge: South End Press Classics, 1998).
4. Lou Waters, "Det. Huserik: Pepper Spray Used on Protesters, Not Tear Gas or Rubber Bullets," "CNN Today," CNN, November 30, 1999. See also Jim Moret and Don Knapp, "Group of Protesters Determined to Tell Side of Story in Seattle With Their Own Means of Communication," "The World Today," CNN, December 2, 1999.
5. Author correspondence with Eric Galatas, August 2001.
6. See details at http://print.indymedia.org/.
7. Author correspondence with Brian Drolet, August 2001.
8. Drolet, August 2001.

THE STRUGGLE AT PACIFICA

Pacifica is the oldest noncommercial radio network in the United States. It began in 1949 and now owns and operates five stations in Berkeley, New York, Washington, D.C., Houston, and Los Angeles and has a number of affiliate stations. Pacifica is the last major non-corporate media network in the United States. It represents an enormous resource. What happens to it is of great import to progressives.

Since the middle of the 1990s, Pacifica has been embroiled in a struggle over conflicting visions about its future. Pacifica should be flourishing. It should be the soil in which we root a progressive media network in the United States. Instead, it has been weakened and compromised. The network has been seized by a board of directors that seems intent on reversing its historic mission of providing progressive and challenging news and information to listeners. The litany of management-instigated firings, bannings, censorship (including the silencing of powerful radio commentaries by Mumia Abu-Jamal), gag rules, and verbal and physical abuse is beyond the pale. The self-selecting Pacifica board, including some members with pro-business, anti-union backgrounds, has presided over decisions that have imperiled the network and have alienated large groups of listeners and supporters.

New York Daily News journalist Juan Gonzalez resigned as co-host of Pacifica's daily nationally syndicated news program "Democracy Now!" shortly after the December 2000 middle-of-the-night "Christmas coup" at WBAI, when three veteran staff were summarily fired without notice or cause. Gonzalez went on the air live on January 31, 2001, and said, "I've come to the conclusion that the Pacifica board has been hijacked by a small clique that has more in common with modern-day corporate vultures than with working-class America." He pointed to the "critical role the network has played in reporting important stories the corporate media ignored, thus helping to shape progressive thought and popular movements throughout the country."[1]

Gonzalez has formed a group called the Pacifica Campaign, which is trying to get control of the board. The campaign has staged rallies, pickets, and e-mail and fax campaigns, and has called for an economic boycott of Pacifica.

Pacifica owns stations and frequencies, a tremendous asset. The Pacifica station in New York, WBAI, and the one in Berkeley, KPFA, are both in the middle of the commercial band. They are worth hundreds of millions of dollars.

In a new book, media scholar Charles Fairchild says that Pacifica's "executive staff and the national board have been engaged in a furious campaign of spin control regarding numerous illegal or unethical actions."[2] He adds, "Pacifica's decisions" related to programming and personnel "seem to be based on what elite technocrats decide is right. Then they extend these processes through the complicated methods of coercion and constraint … that inherently alienate those outside the circles of power."

"Ultimately," Fairchild concludes,

> Pacifica's national board and executive staff have abandoned the goal of fostering the spheres of progressive and democratic discourse

> for which their organization was created and have hidden their agendas behind a vcil of secrecy and obfuscation.[3]

As we are going to press, Gonzalez's co-host Amy Goodman and the other three remaining "Democracy Now!" staff members have endured threats on and off the air by station staff, including a physical assault on Goodman on August 10, 2001. With support from the American Federation of Television and Radio Artists — which agrees that WBAI is not a "safe and appropriate working environment"[4] for "Democracy Now!" — Goodman and her staff have relocated to a studio in Chinatown. As of August 21, she and her small crew were suspended without pay by Pacifica, even as they have continued to produce daily broadcasts.

Pacifica has now lost its most popular and prestigious program and in doing so has further alienated listeners as well as the affiliate stations that paid for and carried "Democracy Now!" Goodman's sign-off since leaving the WBAI studios has become a rallying cry for those trying to save Pacifica:

> We are broadcasting from DCTV, in the historic firehouse of Engine 31 in Chinatown. In the

> midst of a firestorm, what better place to be? In exile from the embattled studios of WBAI, from the studios of the banned and the fired, from the studios of our listeners, I'm Amy Goodman and thanks for listening to another edition of Democracy Now! in Exile.[5]

Goodman is an intrepid and courageous journalist. If we had truly democratic media in this country, everyone would know who she is and her program would be featured on public radio from coast to coast.

The battle for Pacifica is one that progressives must win. But to win it, we have to consider our media activism strategies. We certainly will need to get beyond the choir to reach the congregation. It's crucial that the progressive movement develop a more effective outreach strategy.

How do we move from our cocoon of "cool people" and reach people in the subdivisions, work places, and trailer parks, to talk about issues they want to hear in a language that's meaningful to them without being patronizing, pedantic, or obscure? Millions of people shop at Wal-Mart and Kmart, buy groceries at Safeway and Albertson's, and eat at Burger King and McDonalds. They cannot afford bottled water or organic shiitake mushrooms. We cannot lose sight of them and their role in social change, if we are going to achieve it. This seems to me to be a major task.

Scholar-activist Manning Marable advocates that we use an "inside-outside" strategy. We can't abandon the mainstream media. Where openings exist, we must seize them. Pour in energy and widen the wedges as much as possible. But we also need to create alternative structures to challenge the mainstream media. We need to support publishers like South End, Common Courage, Seven Stories, and other independent efforts. A lot of young people around the country have mastered desktop publishing and are creating 'zines that are highly sophisticated, with imaginative designs and excellent content. One good example is *Clamor*. Another is *Alternative Press Review*.

Creating alternative media is important not only for political reasons, but for psychological ones, as well. Whining and complaining are big turn-offs, particularly to young people. Yes, corporate media and the commercialization of public media are bad. We now have a mountain of evidence to substantiate our thesis. The current media scene is toxic. It should be defined as a public health problem. Its wastes course through our veins. We need to inoculate ourselves. Building new media institutions and expanding existing ones provides therapeutic relief.

I'm optimistic. I think we have to adopt the Gramscian mode of pessimism of the intellect, optimism of the will, and work on finding common ground and taking concrete steps. Step by step you climb the mountain. You can't leap to the top. We have to make a commitment for the long haul. Progressives have to think about running a marathon rather than a sprint. And we need to find ways to overcome sectarian differences, show appreciation, and even express love and compassion for others. Caring is key to building the movement. And, let's not forget, perhaps above all, keeping a sense of humor.

You can do something in your own community. There are lots of projects waiting to be born.

Notes

1 See http://www.pacificacampaign.org/juanresigns.asp.

2 Charles Fairchild, *Community Radio and Public Culture* (Cresskill, New Jersey: Hampton Press, 2001), p. 163.

3 Fairchild, *Community Radio and Public Culture,* pp. 164–65.

4 See Steve Carney, "A New Front in Pacifica's Civil War," *Los Angeles Times,* August 24, 2001, p. 6: 26; Nat Henthoff, "'Democracy Now!' Suspended," *Village Voice,* September

18, 2001. See also the web site for the Pacifica Campaign (Appendix).

5 For information on "Democracy Now! In Exile" visit the Save WBAI web site: http://savewbai.tao.ca/. To listen, visit http://www.democracynow.org/ or WBAI Radio In Exile at http://www.wbix.org.

AFTERWORD

BY MUMIA ABU-JAMAL

Former Minister of Information of the Black Panther Party Eldridge Cleaver once said, "Information is the raw material for new ideas; if you get misinformation, you get some pretty fucked-up ideas."

With late-night lock changes, and a phalanx of security guards prowling the halls, the coup of WBAI-FM, the flagship station of the Pacifica Network, has begun.

Popular veterans of the listener-supported station, like program manager Bernard White and WBAI union shop steward Sharon Harper (both producers of the morning "Wake Up Call" show), received letters of termination at their homes several hours before their shifts were to begin.

WBAI general manager, Valerie Van Isler, who, like White, was a 20-year vet of the station, was similarly fired by Pacifica, ostensibly for failing to accept a position at network headquarters in Washington, D.C.

While these firings were attempts to remove, and thereby install, management personnel, it was also an opening salvo in a pitched battle designed to silence radical dissent, and open the airwaves to the corporatization of WBAI.

If you want WBAI to become a nice, sweet, safe alternative, like NPR, then do nothing. It will happen. If, however, you want to continue to hear about the struggles of the peoples of the world for liberty, for life, for dignity, as in East Timor; or of the noble life and death struggle of the Zapatistas in the mountains of Mexico; or of cases like the slaughter of African immigrant Amadou Diallo; or of the continuing human rights violations occurring every day in the nation's burgeoning prison-industrial complex, then you must fight for it, as you would fight for your very life, or anything dear to you.

The great Frederick Douglass perhaps put it best when he said, "Without struggle there is no progress." If the various communities of New York and northern New Jersey don't struggle for their vision of WBAI-FM, it will be gone. It's as simple as that.

What's happening at 'BAI was attempted a year ago at KPFA-FM in San Francisco. The people of the Bay Area rallied in unprecedented strength — over 10,000 folks at one protest — and backed the Pacifica board down. Listeners to 'BAI must do no less.

In theory at least, the airwaves belong to the people. For the last 40 years, the staff and local management of WBAI have tried to make that theory in America a reality.

If you are thrilled by the no-holds-barred radio reporting of "Democracy Now's" Amy Goodman, who is constantly threatened and harassed by the Pacifica board for her radical reporting, then fight for her.

For in fighting for her, you fight for the finest traditions of WBAI, and against the corporationists who want to turn a national resource into just another commodity.

To keep it raw; to keep it real, you've got to fight for it.

Brief Acknowledgments

Thanks to the indomitable Amy Goodman and Juan Gonzalez for being on the other end of the line, albeit briefly. To those who exist in the dark netherworlds of prison, who listen, and to radicals and revolutionaries worldwide, who fight for change. To Seven Stories — Ona Move! LLJA! maj

APPENDIX

SOME RESOURCES FOR FURTHER INFORMATION

Adbusters Media Foundation
1243 West 7th Avenue
Vancouver BC V6H 1B7
Canada
Phone: (604) 736-9401
Fax: (604) 737-6021
info@adbusters.org
http://www.adbusters.org

Alternative Radio
David Barsamian
PO Box 551
Boulder CO 80306-0551
Phone: (800) 444-1977
Fax: (303) 545-5763
ar@orci.com
http://www.alternativeradio.org

Center for Independent Public Broadcasting
1910 Cochran Road, Manor Oak Two, Suite 441
Pittsburgh PA 15220-1203
Phone: (412) 563-4150
Fax: (412) 563-4960
cipb@cipbonline.org
http://www.cipbonline.org

Center for Media Literacy
3101 Ocean Park Boulevard
Suite 200
Santa Monica CA 90405-3022
Phone: (310) 581-0260
cml@medialit.org
http://www.medialit.org

Commercial Alert
3719 SE Hawthorne Boulevard
Suite 281
Portland OR 97214-5145
Phone: (503) 235-8012
Fax: (503) 235-5073
alert@essential.org
http://www.commercialalert.org

Common Dreams Newscenter
PO Box 443
Portland ME 04112-0443
Phone: (207) 799-2185
Fax: (435) 807-0044
editor@commondreams.org
http://www.commondreams.org

Facets Multimedia
1517 West Fullerton Avenue
Chicago IL 60614-2087
Phone: (773) 281-9075
To order films: (800) 331-6197
http://www.facets.org

Fairness and Accuracy in Reporting (FAIR)
130 West 25th Street, Eighth Floor
New York NY 10001-7406
Phone: (212) 633-6700
Fax: (212) 727-7668
fair@fair.org
http://www.fair.org

FreeSpeech TV
PO Box 6060
Boulder CO 80306-6060
director@freespeech.org
http://www.freespeech.org

Independent Media Center
general@indymedia.org
http://www.indymedia.org/

Institute for Public Accuracy
915 National Press Building
Washington DC 20045-1928
Phone: (202) 347-0020
Fax: (202) 347-0290
dcinstitute@igc.org
http://www.accuracy.org/

Making Contact
National Radio Project
1714 Franklin Street
Suite #100-251
Oakland CA 94612-3409
Phone: (510) 251-1501
Fax: (510) 251-1342
makingcontact@radioproject.org
http://www.radioproject.org

MediaChannel.org
1600 Broadway
Suite 700
New York NY 10019-7413
Phone: (212) 246-0202
Fax: (212) 246-2677
editor@mediachannel.org
http://www.mediachannel.org

Media Education Foundation
26 Center Street
Northampton MA 01060-3027
Phone: (413) 584-8500
To order films: (800) 897-0089
http://www.mediaed.org

Appendix

Media-L
Media Literacy List Serve
http://www.ithaca.edu/looksharp/resources/media-l.html

Media Scope
http://www.mediascope.org

Media Study
http://www.mediastudy.com

Media Watch
PO Box 618
Santa Cruz CA 95061-0618
Phone: (800) 631-6355
mwatch@cruzio.com
http://www.mediawatch.com

Pacifica Campaign
51 MacDougal Street
Suite 80
New York NY 10012-2921
Phone: (800) 797-6229
Fax: (646) 230-9582
pacificacampaign@yahoo.com
http://www.pacificacampaign.org

The Progressive
409 East Main Street
Madison WI 53703-2863
Phone: (608) 257-4626
Fax: (608) 257-3373
circ@progressive.org
http://www.progressive.org/

PR Watch
Center for Media and Democracy

520 University Avenue
Suite 310
Madison WI 53703-4916
Phone: (608) 260-9713
Fax: (608) 260-9714
editor@prwatch.org
http://www.prwatch.org/

Radio for Change
info@radioforchange.com
http://www.workingforchange.com

Z Magazine and Z Net
18 Millfield Street
Woods Hole MA 02543-1122
Phone: (508) 548-9063
Fax: (508) 457-0626
lydia.sargent@zmag.org
http://www.zmag.org

Z Media Institute
18 Millfield Street
Woods Hole MA 02543-1122
Phone: (508) 548-9063
Fax: (508) 457-0626
sysop@zmag.org
http://www.zmag.org

INDEX

Index

Index

Index

Q

R

S

Index

Y

Z

ABOUT THE AUTHOR

David Barsamian lives in Boulder, Colorado, and is the producer of the award-winning syndicated radio program Alternative Radio. A regular contributor to *The Progressive* and *Z* magazine, his most recent interview books include *Eqbal Ahmad: Confronting Empire* (South End Press) and *Propaganda and the Public Mind: Conversations with Noam Chomsky* (South End Press).

For more information on Alternative Radio, visit http://www.alternativeradio.org.

ABOUT SOUTH END PRESS

South End Press is a nonprofit, collectively run book publisher with more than 200 titles in print. Since our founding in 1977, we have tried to meet the needs of readers who are exploring, or are already committed to, the politics of radical social change.

Our goal is to publish books that encourage critical thinking and constructive action on the key political, cultural, social, economic, and ecological issues shaping life in the United States and in the world. In this way, we hope to give expression to a wide diversity of democratic social movements and to provide an alternative to the products of corporate publishing.

For a free catalog, please call 1-800-533-8478, e-mail us at southend@southendpress.org, visit our web site at http://www.southendpress.org., or write to us at: South End Press, 7 Brookline Street, Suite 1, Cambridge, MA 02139-4146. When ordering books, please include $3.50 for postage and handling for the first book and 50 cents for each additional book.